HELP! MY GRANDCHILD HAS A DISABILITY

Dave Deuel

Consulting Editor: Dr. Paul Tautges

Help! My Grandchild Has a Disability

ISBN
Paper: 978-1-63342-161-5
epub: 978-1-63342-162-2
Kindle: 978-1-63342-163-9

Published by **Shepherd Press**
P.O. Box 24
Wapwallopen, PA 18660

www.shepherdpress.com

All Scripture quotations, unless stated otherwise, are from the NIV (2011).

Designed by **documen**

Contents

Introduction: One Family's Story

We were looking for a little peace and stability. I had finished school, gotten married, and taken my first teaching job. We had moved from the East Coast to the West Coast, had our first child, and were preparing for our second. We were also in the process of buying our first home. With changes coming at us at what felt like the speed of light, we yearned for a taste of the quiet life.

No one could have prepared us for what came next.

Early one evening, we drove to the hospital. My wife was in labor with our second child. The nurses welcomed us at the door and seated her in a wheelchair. We joked nervously about a "throne on wheels" fit for a queen. Having turned down the amniocentesis test, due to its risks, we prayerfully anticipated a healthy delivery.

The nurses at Henry-Mayo Newhall Hospital in Santa Clarita, California, were outstanding. They were witty, alert, and light-hearted. Their joking soothed our nerves. The doctor, on the other hand, was all business, as we'd hoped he would be. With the stage set for a perfectly normal birth at an excellent hospital, all was well . . . or so we thought.

When the moment of delivery arrived, I was ready to give our little girl the trendy Laboya bath. This was supposed to soothe the newborn, as it put her back in a state of liquid suspension, simulating a mother's womb. The already focused physician was hypervigilant. Why couldn't he just lighten up a little? Aren't births supposed to be happy occasions? This doctor was stealing our joy! After all, all was well.

But all was not well.

As our sweetheart entered the world, she hardly made a sound. The silence, combined with the looks of panic our doctor gave the nurses, sent a sick feeling to my stomach. Our little girl was in trouble. I was in trouble. What was usually a noisy, happy moment when the pink, squalling little bundle bursts forth making first sounds was a deafening hush. The doctor continued to struggle as he again exchanged glances with the nurses.

Although the delivery team reluctantly allowed

me to do the Laboya bath, I held our baby loosely. She was limp, motionless, and blue. Finally, the team whisked her off to the nursery, or so I thought. No! It was off to the Neonatal Intensive Care Unit (NICU). While they struggled to be polite and sensitive to our feelings, their facial expressions and overall quiet showed clearly that something was wrong. I was getting sicker and sicker in my stomach as my wife rested, unaware that anything was wrong.

That night, I drove home praying, numb and scared. Although I still had no idea what was wrong, I knew for certain we were bracing ourselves for something bad. Exhausted, I dropped off to sleep still nauseated. I no sooner got to sleep when the phone rang. It was my wife. She was crying. "They won't let me see our baby." In a sleep stupor, I recklessly drove several blocks to the hospital and parked in the wrong lot. As I ran through the front door we had entered joyfully just hours earlier, one of the nurses who helped deliver our baby met me. She stammered on the verge of tears, "I need to talk to you about what's going on."

I froze. "We had to take your daughter to the NICU because her heart stopped. We were able to revive her, but she's doing very poorly." Then she said the words I couldn't bear to hear: "She may not live."

I raced to see my little girl. There were so many wires and tubes attached to her that I could hardly find her. I looked up to see the nurse watching my reaction. She covered her mouth and ran for the door, crying. My legs felt like they would buckle. "Lord, not this, please" repeatedly crossed my mind.

Making very little eye contact the doctor repeated the nurse's message, but with much less empathy. "Things are bad. Her heart stopped and we spent twenty minutes resuscitating her. She may not live. If she does live, she may have additional brain damage." The word *additional* hit me like a freight train. It was final. The only thing we knew for certain was that our little girl had some sort of brain damage. That point was certain. The doctor also told us that if we wanted to confirm the diagnosis we would need to do a chromosome test. I had no idea what he was talking about.

After two weeks of waiting, the first chromosome test was thrown out due to accidental contamination. When we were asked if we wanted to do another test, I impatiently responded, "No, you're not putting my little girl through that again." So we moved forward with no clear genetic testing, only a cluster of symptoms that characterized Down syndrome. Our hearts ached.

Down syndrome. I hated those words. What I hated worse was *Down's baby*, or just *Down's*. I wanted *up*.

Our pediatrician called several weeks later and said in broken English, "Your baby is trisomy 21." Thinking there must be language confusion, I asked impatiently, "What did you say?" She responded, "Your baby is trisomy 21, sir, Down syndrome." The mind-numbing last two words required no explanation. Several of my family members involved in special education often referred to kids in their classes as having Down syndrome. In the vernacular of a former generation, I was the father of a retarded child, or as some would say, a "Mongoloid baby." That cut deep. What responsible human being would come up with such a title? What sensitive society would use it?

Several thousand miles away from family, alone and crushed, we tried to move forward with life. At church, people genuinely tried to encourage us. One woman asked sympathetically, "Do you plan to keep her?" My first thought was, "Well, what else would I do with her?" Someone explained later that the previous generation was encouraged to institutionalize children "like this." "Like what?" I fired back. I had entered the world of language hypersensitivity. I was taking a nose dive.

My mind kept wandering to verses like:

> *Children are a heritage from the* LORD.
>
> *(Psalm 127:3)*

All children? Maybe not some children. And then there was another verse:

> *Take delight in the* LORD,
> *and he will give you the desires of your heart.*
>
> *(Psalm 37:4)*

What I desired was a normal, healthy baby. These verses were not working for me. The confusion was overwhelming. In a particularly dark moment, life seemed like it was over.

But life was not over. A bright new day had dawned for my entire family, although it would take a while for us to realize it. God's gift of acceptance would ease the pain and keep us going. But that would take some time and personal growth.

Today my daughter Joanna is thirty years old, healthy and quite happy. As a family, our lives are rich with God's grace. Daily, we experience great contentment. My other three kids (who have compassion ahead of their years) dote over their sister and enrich her life. God *has* given us the desires of our hearts: children, all children, are a gift from the Lord. His mercy lifts parents and grandparents up and carries them over every rough road. And his light breaks through the darkness.

I share my family's story because I believe that our experience is not unusual for families into which God places a child with a disability. What might be unusual, however, is the role grandparents and surrogate grandparents have played, and continue to play, in the life of my daughter and the rest of my family. So what is the role of Christian grandparents in the life of a grandchild with a disability? That's what this mini-book is about.

1 What Is a Biblical Grandparent?

The day your first grandchild was born you were not invited to consider grandparenting; suddenly you *were* a grandparent. That's because grandparenting is a calling. Callings are not freely chosen. In the truest sense, callings are imposed on us. They are not sought, found, or discovered; they are answered.[1] At first, this arrangement may not sound inviting. In fact, you may feel trapped. But just as God gives us our mission in life, so he also resources and trains us to do the work well. He can even give us an unexpected desire to love and care for a child that emboldens our hearts. But calling has another characteristic which may surprise us: we will never retire from our calling. In his book *The Call*, Os Guinness writes,

> *God calls men and women who will be committed to their life tasks with no reservations, no retreats, no regrets.*[2]

This is true for all Christians, but is especially important to remember when disability enters our families. More on this later.

The needs of grandchildren and their parents help define the grandparent's role. Grandchildren are royal blessings. Proverbs 17:6 tells us,

> *Children's children are a crown to the aged.*

But what if your crown is not what you expected? What if your grandchild has a disability? This mini-book offers grandparents their honored place as kings and queens in their families. If the Lord has blessed you with a grandchild who has a disability, then roll up your sleeves and get ready to polish that precious and beautiful crown!

Parenting a child with a disability can be a blessing. Grandparenting a child with a disability can be a delight! As the parent of a thirty-year-old young lady who is blessed by two sets of godly grandparents, I have discovered that grandparents can make a crucial difference. Let me explain what I have learned from Scripture and from how my daughter's grandparents illustrate its principles.

Accepting Your Role

In many ways, grandparenting a child who has a disability is like grandparenting a child who does not. But there are unique blessings and challenges which come with grandparenting (and parenting) kids with disabilities. I'm primarily writing to grandparents, but I want parents to hear this conversation as well, because interchange between these two family roles is important. In short, grandparents must *respect* the role of parents, while parents must *accept* the role of grandparents.

In order to understand family relational roles in the Bible, we must first understand the biblical home. In the Old Testament the home was called "the house of the father." The father's house was made up of what we refer to today as the *nuclear family* as well as extended family, including aunts, uncles, and cousins. This is important to grasp, since Jesus describes heaven this way:

> *My Father's house has many rooms.*
> *(John 14:2)*

In Bible times, when a young couple married, the family would often build an additional room on the father's house for them. Yes, they were one big, happy family! Because the grandparents were the oldest surviving family members in the home, they played a critical role. Scripture was the fountainhead of all learning and the grandparents were the living examples. The example of deceased relatives also played a significant role as it lived on through the stories grandparents told the family. Deceased ancestors lived and spoke through the stories of grandparents. Life in the house of the father was very good!

Psalm 128 compares a blessed home to an olive tree with little shoots springing up and surrounding it. The imagery speaks vividly to the gift of children in the home. But the psalmist goes on to describe a fruitful home as one in which parents see their children's children (verse 6). And seeing involves much more than domestic bliss. On the one hand, living to see your grandchildren is an indescribable blessing; on the other, it is a call to fulfill grandparental duties which will entail hardship. No wonder Martin Luther called Psalm 128 a psalm of comfort for those who experience challenges in the home.[3] The psalm also reminds us that not all people will be able to have children. Those of us who do will be blessed all the more to see our grandchildren be born and grow up to maturity.

In the home in Bible times, campfires became story times about God's goodness to Israel's families. Children asked questions of their aged grandparents, and their answers would live on for a lifetime in the children's memories. No wonder one of the greatest blessings Job received after his painful ordeal was to see his grandchildren born and grow (Job 42:16)!

A brief refresher on family life in biblical times gives us more insight.

A Supportive Relationship and Role

What were family relationships like in ancient Israel? Since three or more generations lived under one roof in close proximity, all behavior and words were on display for the rest of the family to see and hear. Although this had its advantages, it could also present challenges. Is it any wonder that when the church was born, it was immediately likened to a family dwelling together in God's house, "the household of faith" (Galatians 6:10, ESV), working together for the good of all? In such a context the role of grandparents within the larger family unit became crucial. After all, the grandparents not only were the repository of family wealth and history, but they also would pass on these treasures to the surviving generations at their death.

How were families provided for and protected? Circles of family and friends provided protection and prosperity. Grandparents fit ideally into that broad framework of supportive relationships.

Grandchildren with disabilities are like everyone else in that they need a circle of support. It might be helpful to view the family of a child with a disability as a series of concentric circles. Grandparents are in the third circle, parents in the second, and the child in the center. Like protective and providing agents, grandparents surround the nuclear family of which they are a part. Outside of the nuclear family are multiple circles of friends.

We need a house, a home, and a family. We learn from the home context in Scripture that children with disabilities need these as well. The house provides protection and privacy for the child with a disability and his or her family. The home, a legal and social institution, offers the privileges and responsibilities that all families need. Family members need to love others and be loved by others, not just as individuals but as entire families. When marriages and funerals occur, families unite in celebration and in sorrow. The family lives and thrives in the house as a home. Children with disabilities can grow and flourish here.

But in ancient Israel, in the absence of grandparents, others could stand in—and the same is true today.

Surrogate Grandparenting

Where there are no grandparents living in close proximity, the Lord may provide surrogate grandparents. For us, a busy pastor's family with four kids, life was a blur at church, as you might expect. Like most families, we entered the door of the church and scattered in six directions. I led the service and preached, and my wife played the piano. This was not an ideal situation for parents of a child with a disability! Seeing our distress, Mrs. Smith offered to care for our disabled daughter during the service. During the communion service, which I led and for which my wife played the piano, Mrs. Smith asked my daughter if she believed in Jesus. Characteristically, Joanna responded "Yes." If Joanna seemed a little confused, Mrs. Smith would explain the gospel to her as a refresher. As I watched all of this happening (from the pulpit!) in real time, I would silently pray, "Lord, thank you for Mrs. Smith,

Joanna's surrogate grandmother." Mr. Smith, a very clever wood carver, carved Disney characters out of wood and painted them for Joanna. We have those to this day. As you've probably concluded, the Smiths were not only surrogate grandparents for Joanna—they were surrogate parents for my wife and me as we wrestled with the challenges of life. To this day, they remain close friends, even at a distance.

Both parents and grandparents must love unconditionally like God. In a world that rewards good behavior and punishes bad, it is easy to place conditions on love. Loving someone becomes a reward for that person loving you. But God doesn't place those kinds of conditions on his love. Loving unconditionally over long distances can be a challenge. If personal conflicts develop, it is more difficult to resolve them if you cannot talk face-to-face or if they get lost amidst the hectic pace of life. These factors make grandparenting more challenging, but technology makes it possible to stay fully and visually engaged with family over the miles and through the craziness. However, there is no substitute for a family visit whenever possible, especially the cherished once-a-year summer vacation or holiday gathering.

Tricky Questions

Answering several deeper questions takes us to the heart of grandparenting.

- *Whose child is it?* This tricky question receives a lot of interesting answers. The simple answer is that a child belongs to God. God entrusts parents with their children. Grandparents are first and foremost entrusted with their own children who are now parents themselves. This means that individuals or couples who were great parents may not necessarily be outstanding grandparents. It raises another important question.
- *Who is responsible for raising the child?* Based on Scripture, the answer is both parents and grandparents, within their respective roles. But having similar responsibilities does not equal having similar roles. Parents should parent children. Unless grandparents have stepped into parental roles due to death or other circumstances, grandparents have another role to play.

» *What role should grandparents play, then?* First, grandparents should support the parents in their role. This may be a learning curve for some because most of us typically want to treat our grandchildren like our children—that is, we naturally want to participate as parents. After all, we have had a great deal of practice raising our own children, and our children (our grandchildren's parents) should recognize that we are the family authorities on raising kids. But this is a potentially dangerous assumption which can cause problems for the parents and grandchildren. Should grandparents have a role in raising their grandchildren? Unquestionably, yes. In fact, ignoring your grandchildren is a dereliction of duty assigned by God. But what specifically should characterize the role of grandparents in the lives of their children as parents and of their grandchildren? In his study *Biblical Grandparenting*, Josh Mulvihill argues that at least four profiles characterize how grandparents should view themselves: encouraging voice, supportive partner, loving friend, and disciple-maker.[4]

Responding to Disability

When Jim and Marge's daughter gave birth to a girl with Down syndrome, they struggled with what they should do. How would they talk to their daughter and her husband? How would the birth of this child affect the lives of their daughter's other two children whom Jim and Marge adored? How would they ever be able to tell this little darling about Jesus so that she could believe? Could she possibly understand the gospel? Or would it be too complex for her? Would she have medical issues? How long would she live? Would life ever be the same as it was before the birth of this precious child? All Jim and Marge could think to do was pray, "Help! Our grandchild has a disability."

Families can respond poorly to disability. Not surprisingly, we might view disability as a threat. Disability itself is not a threat, but our response to it could be. Although surveys have been conducted on the effects of disability on divorce rates, results are inconclusive. What we do know is that the parents of a child with disability face greater stress in their lives than those of children who have no disability. This can and often does affect their marriage. Why? One obvious reason is that the pressures become all-consuming. The disability may claim the couple's time, energy, and resources. Freedom feels lost. If they are not careful, the needs of the disability can overwhelm them. It fills all of the empty spaces in their lives. They lose their reserves. Joy seems to run out. But that does not need to be the end.

In fact, wrestling with disability can draw couples closer together. Their marriage may become stronger and more resilient as by God's grace the disability builds their stamina and strength. But the sad fact is that some marriages become so depleted that couples see no way out except through divorce. One reason this happens is because they never developed strategies to manage stress. Disability will either force the issue and, in so doing, become a significant contributor to stress on a marriage, or it will lead them to rely more heavily on the Lord.

So what can grandparents do? Grandparents can become marital and home support for their adult children and their grandchildren. But how can this be done? Several suggestions for how grandparents can help parents of a child with a disability through their dark nights form the subject of our next chapter.

2 What Should Biblical Grandparents Do?

Have you seen the bumper sticker that says, "We're spending our children's inheritance"? Parents committed to Scripture should change that slogan to: "Our children *are* our inheritance" (see Psalm 127:3 KJV). This applies equally to grandparenting. We receive grandchildren from the Lord as an inheritance, and we give them back to our family, church, and community to fulfill their calling—God's plan for their lives. In both our receiving and our giving, our children and grandchildren are our inheritance.

Another popular cliché says, "Children don't come with a user's manual." But this is not true for Christians. We have a manual for all of life. Scripture speaks clearly to the roles of parents and grandparents.

Some General Guidelines

What grandparents do should be an outworking of who they are. By God's design, they are grandparents. But this is not just a role; it is a relationship. Ideally, the grandparents must be committed to Jesus Christ, first and foremost. This need not mean they must be pastors or other vocational ministry workers. Rather, it means they must be deeply committed to their grandchildren and seek to have a spiritual impact on their hearts and lives. Given that spiritual priority, what are some ways that grandparents can act on these commitments?

1. *Start with the basics*. Raise your grandchild "in the training and instruction of the Lord" (Ephesians 6:4). Some will object, saying that this is the work of parents alone. But that is the point. Your supportive role as a grandparent of a child with a disability largely entails supporting the work of the parents, and encouraging both the parents and your grandchildren in the Lord.

2. *Continue what you have begun.* Grandparenting a child with a disability began when you first formed relationships with the child's parents (your child and his or her spouse) and set the tone for working together. That may have gone well. On the other hand, you may be starting out your grandparenting role with relational deficits. If you are at odds with your child and his or her spouse, you will find it challenging to be an effective grandparent. God expects believers to take the necessary steps toward reconciliation and healing (Matthew 5:23–24; Romans 12:18). Just as your automobile needs a front-end alignment in order for you to be able to steer it properly, so you may need to focus first on biblical family alignment before your grandparenting role is well received. What better time than now to make these adjustments and corrections?

3. *Improve at grandparenting.* Before you attempt to be a good grandparent of a child with a disability, first strive just to be a good grandparent. Individuals who are struggling with being a good grandparent in general will find it more difficult or confusing to

grandparent a child with a disability. For this reason, the lessons drawn out in the first chapter will guide you toward becoming a better grandparent.

4. *Prepare for the stresses that accompany disability.* Here moms and dads may respond differently. Moms often become so consumed with caring for a child with a disability that they find it more difficult to keep up with other family duties. Dads find intensive childcare confusing and daunting. Therefore, support both parents, especially the dad. Dads are often conspicuously absent from homes into which the Lord has placed a child with a disability. I am reminded of Bill, whose wife bore a daughter with Down syndrome when the couple were in their early fifties. At first, Bill was not only a good dad, he was nearly bionic. He doted over his precious little daughter with seemingly endless energy. Suddenly, though, everything changed. Bill left his wife and daughter for another woman in what seemed like a day. Bill ran. And he kept running. Grandparents, beware. Husbands sometimes get lost in the confusion of

disability, and wives get worn out. Don't deny or ignore these stresses. Address them one at a time, sweeping nothing under the carpet. I highly recommend another mini-book in this series, *Help! Disability Pressures Our Marriage*, by Dr. Ernie Baker.

5. *Provide for your children and grandchildren.* Proverbs 13:22 says, "A good person leaves an inheritance for their children's children." Although your family will appreciate any financial gifts you give them, the greatest provision for your grandchildren will not be material wealth, but biblical wealth or instruction. Leaving your grandchild with a godly example to remember is a priceless gift. However, financial help still plays a significant role in making the lives of grandchildren better, particularly grandchildren with disabilities. For example, my wife's parents were extraordinarily wise to set up a trust for their other daughter who is now in her sixties. Since she has an intellectual disability from a high fever associated with the malaria she contracted when her family served as missionaries, she cannot provide for herself. But if my sister-

in-law does not need all of the trust money, it will pass to my thirty-year-old daughter (my sister-in-law's niece and their granddaughter) when my sister-in-law goes to be with the Lord. This, I believe, is what the writer of Proverbs had in mind when he wrote about this special way grandparents can care for their grandchildren many years after the former have gone to be with the Lord. It will take careful thinking on your part to leave wealth that won't be squandered, or worse, used to harm your grandchild and those around him or her. What is more, we must understand that helping our grandchildren believe in Jesus, and grow spiritually, are prioritized in Scripture over providing them with an endless supply of spending money or leaving them wealth at our deaths.

6. *Bless your grandchildren.* A blessing is a wish in the form of a prayer. For example, Genesis 31:55 says of Laban: "Early the next morning Laban kissed his grandchildren and his daughters and blessed them. Then he left and returned home." Laban realized he might never see them again. That made this prayer extra special. Imagine praying for

your children and grandchildren as they go off to the mission field, not knowing if you will ever see them again. This kind of prayer summons God to bless them based on his covenant-keeping faithfulness.

The following suggestions about how you can be a blessing to your grandchild with a disability may be worth considering:

- With disability, always put the child first, not the disability. But do so without creating a child-centered family. The disability is what God has given; but the child is the inheritance.
- Lead your family, friends, and acquaintances in how they should treat your grandchild. If they feel awkward at first, they won't after getting to know your grandchild.
- Redirect the sadness of disability toward the joy of heaven. This may be difficult at first. But those who thrive with a child with a disability are those who see God's glass for their lives as being half-full. The alternative perspective (half-empty) is very harmful, even if no one intends to be gloomy.

In general, the Bible tells us to raise children

with disabilities as we would those without them. But it is in matters of the heart that grandparents will be most supportive to their precious grandchildren. For this reason, grandparents must give careful attention to training their grandchild for life with a disability. Not surprisingly, this will largely require a spiritual focus.

Important Truths for Training Grandchildren

Of all the responsibilities grandparents have, they would do well to recognize that they have a unique opportunity to teach. Due to their age, the respect due them, and the opportunities for relaxed conversation with them, grandparents can informally instruct their beloved grandchildren in ways no one else can. The following suggestions may prove helpful.

1. *Embrace Jesus Christ by faith.* The greatest gift grandparents can give their grandchild is their personal testimony to the saving grace of Jesus Christ. The way we love our grandchildren best is by telling them the gospel, which we ourselves must believe. Scripture tells us that before we ever sinned,

we were born sinners. David says, "Surely I was sinful at birth, sinful from the time my mother conceived me" (Psalm 51:5). As grandparents, we can lovingly and gently explain that "the wages of sin is death, but the gift of God is eternal life in Christ Jesus our Lord" (Romans 6:23). The goal in sharing the good news of Jesus is not to scare our grandchildren, but to make them aware of what Jesus has done and why it was necessary for our eternal salvation. It is only through Jesus and his finished work on the cross that our sin, and our grandchildren's sin, can be forgiven by God. We can be delivered from eternal judgment only through Jesus, for "salvation is found in no one else" (Acts 4:12). Jesus died on the cross for sinners, and rose from the dead. As we embrace Christ for our own need, and share our personal testimony of faith with our grandchildren, they can be helped to understand and respond to Christ's love for themselves.

2. *Understand Israel's John 3:16.* The Old Testament equivalent to John 3:16 is Exodus 34:6–7, which says, "The LORD, the LORD, the compassionate and gracious God, slow to anger, abounding in love and faithfulness, maintaining love to thousands, and forgiving wickedness, rebellion and sin." The psalmist applies this message, describing God's character to grandparents and grandchildren: "But from everlasting to everlasting the LORD's love is with those who fear him, and his righteousness with their children's children" (Psalm 103:17). Your grandchild with a disability needs an accurate and full picture of who God is and how he can sustain him or her through the disability.

3. *Teach your grandchildren well.* God gave the pattern for a grandparent's instruction in Deuteronomy 6 with the goal that grandchildren might fear the Lord (Deuteronomy 6:2; see also 4:9). Through grandparents' teaching one-to-one and talking about God's instruction in all places

and at all times (6:7), their grandchildren will learn to love the Lord with all their heart, soul, and might (6:5). This passage underscores the need to show grandchildren how God's law applies to all situations in life. In fact, Deuteronomy gives us a sequence of actions that starts with *reading* and *hearing* God's law, and then moves to *learning* and *fearing* God and *worshipping* only him. Only then will they be prepared for *doing* God's law and ultimately *teaching* it to others by following the same pattern. What first may appear like a complex process turns out to be a sacred sequence leading to spiritual growth.[5] We would do well to be conscious of it in our teaching and our learning.

4. *Remember that good instruction will come through the spoken word and an exemplary life.* The Israelite young were to seek wisdom from the older family members in the home, especially the grandparents. The grandparents were to make their counsel available, but not to force it on their children or their grandchildren. This impulse is described by the psalmist:

He decreed statutes for Jacob
and established the law in Israel,
which he commanded our ancestors
to teach their children,
so the next generation would know them,
even the children yet to be born,
and they in turn would tell their children.
Then they would put their trust in God
and would not forget his deeds
but would keep his commands.
(*Psalm 78:5–7*)

Teaching in the book of Proverbs moves from passive listening and learning to active doing.[6] In fact, the teacher's role was not to load down the child with pages of information but to create the conditions in which the child would want to learn of the teacher's own motivation.[7] A teacher's primary role was to help students want to learn. No wonder the church father Augustine of Hippo, who taught on the principles and methods of learning, confidently said, "Free curiosity has greater power to stimulate learning than rigorous coercion."[8]

5. *Be there and available.* Some grandparents decide to retire and move to vacation-like surroundings. "We've earned it," they say. But does retirement absolve you of the blessings and responsibilities of being a grandparent? Some grandparents are running away just as their kids once did when they wanted to escape a strict home!
6. *Tell family stories about God.* The psalmist tells us, "One generation commends your works to another; they tell of your mighty acts" (Psalm 145:4). Whereas we might start our stories like this: "Let me tell you about the time Uncle John did such-and-such . . .," according to Scripture the Israelite children would ask, "What do these stones mean?" when they encountered a monument, and "Why do we celebrate this holiday?" on Passover. Some stories started out with "Our fathers told us . . ." You may want to be cautious about overdoing your storytelling. If you find your family members saying, "Here we go again!" it's likely you are abusing your storytelling role. And, as in Scripture, God should always be the hero of the story.[9]

7. *Teach about spiritual matters concretely.* The relational closeness of families provides the fertile soil for spiritual one-to-one ministry. On my daughter Joanna's eighth birthday, a friend showed up at the door with a balloon bouquet for her. After I had handed Joanna the balloons, I stood in our front doorway and talked to the friend for a few minutes. When I had finished talking I could not at first find Joanna. When I eventually found her outside, I noticed that the balloons were nowhere in sight. I asked Joanna where they were. Her response, in characteristic broken syntax, was, "Balloon, sky, Jesus." As I looked up, I could see the balloons ascending in the sky, inevitably on their way to heaven, where we had taught Joanna that Jesus lives.
8. *Be a good listener.* So much of what grandparents do involves speaking and instructing. But one of the most important ministries a grandparent can have is careful listening. Listening is not passively saying nothing. Good listening will involve asking questions, particularly the kind that reveal what is wrong and how a grandparent can help. But much of our listening attempts

to control the conversation. When parents face the realities of their child having a disability, they need someone to talk to who will listen. Pastors will play a critical role in meeting this need, but parents also need family members to hear what they have to say. Many yearn just to have an open conversation about their child with a disability so that they can know how family members feel. All too often, families choose to avoid the topic of a child's disability because it seems unpleasant, even hurtful, to the parents and the child. But the fact is that those parents want to discuss the child's disability, and maybe even want to ask for the help that only a family member can give. Daughters need to talk openly with their mothers, and sons with their fathers. Avoiding the topic can turn the disability into a social stigma, an embarrassment to the entire family. Such a misunderstanding needs to be laid to rest. If families can do this together, the parents of a child with a disability will be better prepared to integrate into the church and broader community.

Kevin, an active ten-year-old, was being bullied in school due to his disability. A group of boys verbally and sometimes physically abused him, particularly in physical education class. Because of his disability, Kevin was not athletic. Instead, he preferred doing art or playing music on his French horn in the school band. But the abuse was escalating and Kevin no longer wanted to leave his room, much less go to school. Kevin's parents both worked long hours and found it hard to spend time with him and his sister. They had little understanding of what was going on in Kevin's life. As a result, the problem fell to his grandfather, Fred, who had noticed the discouragement in his grandson's eyes. After a particularly difficult day in school, Fred asked Kevin, in kindness and gentleness, how he was doing. At first, Kevin did not want to discuss his problem with his grandfather. He was ashamed and felt like a little child crying out for coddling. But Fred displayed the wisdom of Proverbs 20:5 and he knew how to draw out Kevin's fears by telling him about the time he himself was bullied in school. This opened the door for Kevin to share his fear of the bullies and his shame at being around other kids in his class. It also set the stage for Fred to listen carefully and ask leading questions about who was doing the bullying. They ended their conversation by praying that God would provide Kevin with wisdom to deal with the bullies by winning their friendship. This would not have happened if Fred had not first determined to become a good listener.

A Spiritual Legacy

Entrust God's truth to your grandchild like treasure. Ensure that the family embraces the pattern of truth for the next generation. An unspoken assumption for perpetuating the truth is that grandparents are not only repositories of biblical wisdom, but they also must take steps to support the passing on of that wisdom to the next generation. Paul underscores this when he says to Timothy,

And the things you have heard me say in the presence of many witnesses entrust to

> *reliable people who will also be qualified to teach others.*
>
> (*2 Timothy 2:2*)

A wonderful example of godly grandparenting is Lois, Timothy's grandmother. Scripture commemorates her for reading and teaching Scripture to her grandson, who grew up to be a pastor. Paul's argument to Timothy is: repeat the pattern of your mother and grandmother (2 Timothy 1:5), and

> *What you heard from me, keep as the pattern of sound teaching, with faith and love in Christ Jesus.*
>
> (*2 Timothy 1:13*)

We must note that the women in the family taught Timothy first, before the Apostle Paul did. Some like to refer to this process as leaving a "spiritual legacy." But we should note that the truth taught and embraced is not the legacy left by a parent to a child; it is the repository of truth begun in the home and continued in the church. No one person or institution may lay claim to this legacy. It is shared. And it is timeless.

3 What Should Biblical Grandparents *Not* Do?

While there are many things grandparents can do to love and serve their grandchild with a disability and to support the parents in their responsibilities, there are also things they should *not* do. For example:

1. *Do not interfere.* Intervene only in a crisis. Sooner or later, all family relationships experience conflict. If one party is your adult child, you may be tempted to voice your opinion or offer a helpful insight. This can be very risky and is potentially damaging, particularly when it comes to taking sides. The better choice is to listen quietly or even to leave the room. The sage reminds us, "To answer before listening—that is folly and shame" (Proverbs 18:13). You can always talk to the individual later when the contesting party is no longer around.

Even then, do not succumb to the perilous choice of micromanaging your adult child's relationships, particularly with his or her spouse or children.

2. *Do not harm grandchild's view of God.* Never harm the faith of your grandchildren (Psalm 73:15), but instead tell stories of God's faithfulness in your family (Psalm 73:28). Talk about the Lord at all times (Deuteronomy 6:7). This applies to parents as well as grandparents. Rather than being preachy, let your conversation be seasoned with the Lord's grace. Be grateful for all that the Lord has given you and talk about it. Understand the biblical view of disability and teach it to your children or grandchildren. As a senior, you may have a disability that will help you build a rapport with your grandchild: "Grandma has a disability and so do I."
3. *Don't go against parents' ground rules.* Some grandparents joke about their role by saying, "We just spoil our grandkids rotten and then send them home for their parents to fix." If this sounds funny in conversation,

it can be perilous in real time. Children thrive when parents and grandparents follow the same ground rules. Without consistency, they become confused and frustrated. This type of frivolous joking can make a grandparent's efforts toward helping counterproductive. It reminds us of the warning, "The words of the reckless pierce like swords" (Proverbs 12:18).

Poor Examples

What are some examples of poor grandparenting? Noah demonstrated the folly of drunkenness when he exposed his nakedness to his sons. The punishment for that sin was passed down as a curse to his grandchildren and later generations of descendants (Genesis 9:20–29). Achan disobeyed God by stealing some of the spoils of battle that the Lord won when he destroyed Jericho. Achan's grandchildren were stoned along with the rest of the family because of their grandfather's greed (Joshua 7). King Saul was a devastating grandfather to his grandson Mephibosheth, who became disabled when a nurse dropped him as a child (2 Samuel 4:4). Even as a former king of Israel, Saul left no appreciable inheritance for his grandson, nor did he leave the customary plot of land for his grandson to farm. Most tragically, Saul left his grandson a shameful legacy of his disobedience to God.

By contrast, King David, most of whose children died due to David's sin with Bathsheba as well as their own unwise choices, became a surrogate grandparent to Saul's grandson (see 2 Samuel 9). An unnoticed detail of the David and Mephibosheth story is that David made it possible for Mephibosheth to work, provide food for himself and perhaps David's house, and earn an income. He even gave Mephibosheth Saul's territory which David rightfully owned.[10] David did not spoil Mephibosheth with charity and care. Using his own honor and authority the king gave him a respectable place at the family table to preserve Mephibosheth's dignity. Not only does the account of David and Mephibosheth provide us with a good example of grandparenting, it also reminds us that we, too, can be foster grandparents to a child whose grandparents have passed away or live at a distance, or who have chosen not to be involved in their grandchild's life.

Sadly, many grandchildren are effectively abandoned by their grandparents because the child has a disability. Some of us may not have grandchildren. But we can all be surrogate grandparents and “adopt” a grandchild with a disability.

4 How Can Biblical Grandparents Prepare for the Future?

In the last Bible book he wrote, King Solomon exhorts us this way:

> *Remember your Creator*
> *in the days of your youth,*
> *before the days of trouble come*
> *and the years approach when you will say,*
> *"I find no pleasure in them."*
>
> (Ecclesiastes 12:1)

In poetic form, he goes on to describe the physical deterioration of old age (Ecclesiastes 12:2–8). This reminds us that our days will become more difficult as time marches on, and life will become more challenging physically and mentally. This is just one more reason why you should seize every moment you have to be a blessing to your grandchildren. The future is uncertain. Here are some ways to do that.

1. *Accept the Lord's care for you as you age.* "Even to your old age and gray hairs I am he, I am he who will sustain you. I have made you and I will carry you; I will sustain you and I will rescue you" (Isaiah 46:4). Do not reject the measure of strength that God gives you in your older years. Embrace the Lord's commitment to you and your grandchildren: "But from everlasting to everlasting the LORD's love is with those who fear him, and his righteousness with their children's children" (Psalm 103:17). If your grandchild understands that roughly 80 percent of us will become disabled in our older years, he or she may become more comfortable with his or her own disability.

2. *Enjoy and relish your crown.* An old king once wrote, "Children's children are a crown to the aged" (Proverbs 17:6). How are grandchildren a crown to grandparents? Just having grandchildren is viewed as a blessing, a crown. When you look at a picture of your grandchildren, what do you see? Crowns are bestowed. Crowned grandparents didn't win the lottery. It's better than that. They have received gifts sent from God.

3. *Honor and celebrate old age.* At a time in history and in a culture that disdains old age, Christians must think differently and resist the status quo. God commands the younger to honor those who are older for good reason. Older individuals have gained valuable wisdom through studying God's Word and accumulating positive and negative feedback from all of life's experiences. This is the formula for wisdom! Gray heads do not need to be dyed, and aging skin does not need multiple surgeries or "fountain of youth" products to hide the effects of age. Show it. Live it. Celebrate old age. And let us feel sadness for younger people who reject the wisdom of life for the foolishness of independence and individual freedom. They will learn; it needs to come through the school of hard knocks and personal failures. Embrace the pattern of older Christians instructing the younger described in Titus 2:1–8.

4. *Be patient.* Grandparenting, if it is to be done well, will be challenging and will require great wisdom. It also demands patience. The heart of a child is changed

no more easily than an adult's, and with no less dependence on God's grace. Parents and grandparents cannot download a doctrinal statement or a catechism into their children's or grandchildren's hearts. Children—even the most compliant—need changed hearts.[11] We sometimes hear new parents saying, "The trouble with giving birth for the first time is that newborns do not come with a manual." As we have said, this is not true. God has given us a manual in Scripture. But the fact is, God has provided new parents with another manual of mediated Scripture in their own parents. They are repositories of trial and error, but, if they know the Lord, their experience is seasoned with Scripture. In short, the spiritual resources described in this minibook are available to those who have acknowledged their sinful condition and put their faith in Jesus Christ as their Savior. Some of this counsel may be helpful to non-Christians. But a Christian grandparent is the best resource a child, or his or her parent, can have.

5. *Make music as a family.* As my family's historian, I often receive keepsakes and relics from aged family members. In my office, I have a tambourine, banjo, and mandolin, all of which were owned and played by my ancestors in family bands. That's right: my family enjoyed making music together. What is more, on the inside of the tambourine are written the lyrics of songs they sang, along with special dates. These treasured instruments remind me that my family made music together for one another. This is a picture of the family solidarity needed to grandparent a child with a disability. And you, as the grandparent, have the privilege of leading.

Conclusion

Grandparents, particularly grandfathers, need to reject the modern message about a long and relaxing retirement. Some grandparents will find themselves saying, "But I am old and I've been looking forward to retirement; I've worked hard and earned it!" If God has placed a grandchild with a disability into your family, I encourage you to rethink that plan. Do you want to seek relaxation, striving to find enjoyment in vacuous things that, in the words of Ecclesiastes, are like "chasing after the wind?" Or would you rather support your child and his or her spouse as they raise your precious grandchild? Shouldn't your commitment to support and love look like the psalmist's description: "They will still bear fruit in old age, they will stay fresh and green" (Psalm 92:14)? Like trees planted near streams that bear fresh fruit, grandparents whose delight is in the law of the Lord and who meditate on his law day and night will flourish into their final days (Psalm 1).

The admonition to "number our days" (Psalm 90:12) does not mean that we should count our days, but rather we should make them count. Don't give up your crown for a few short-lived moments of recreational pleasure. Life does not owe you a retirement; God offers you a full and satisfying life. Consider viewing retirement as redeployment, having more time to fulfill God's calling. Invest the remaining time that God has given you into your grandchildren and their parents. Your treasure will be waiting for you in heaven. The fact is, your greatest treasure is the grandchild who needs your spiritual encouragement and example right now. Don't squander it on trinkets or expensive experiences. In all things, remember the words of our Lord:

> *For where your treasure is, there your heart will be also.*
>
> *(Matthew 6:21)*

What about leaving a legacy? Do not spend a lot of unnecessary time thinking and talking about this. Instead, keep your focus on one goal: to be memorable, particularly to the grandchild with a disability whom you adore. Rather than leaving a great deal of wealth or a famous reputation, leave your grandchildren a legacy that will impact them for spiritual growth and for eternity. Your faith and faithfulness lived out before those little crowns will be your only lasting legacy. Don't settle for less. Pass it on.

Personal Application Projects

1. Read Psalm 103:1–18. Take note of verse 17, which encourages grandparents to remember that their own righteousness and faith will not be forgotten. Verse 2 exhorts us not to forget the Lord's benefits. The way not to forget is to actively remember. What are some stories of the Lord's faithfulness you can tell to your grandchild with a disability? These may include:

- » Specific answers to prayer, or ways the Lord was faithful to lead you.
- » People in your family who have demonstrated great faith and faithfulness—not only those who went into full-time Christian ministry, but also those who found their calling in life and lived out their faith in the community.
- » Family members who have endured suffering and found God's wisdom and strength to go on.

One story that I tell my children is about family members who have failed, but who learned from their mistakes and went on to find great success in their calling.

2. Read Luke 11:2–4. In response to the disciples' request "Lord, teach us to pray," Jesus instructed them. John the Baptist did the same with his disciples. Consider the privilege of teaching your grandchild with a disability to pray. Perhaps begin to help your grandchild accept your spiritual nurture by asking if you can pray with them about a current problem. When you finish praying, assure your grandchild you will continue to pray for them. Then, when you see them again, remind them that you have been praying, and ask how the problem has progressed since you started praying about it. Even if the problem is not resolved, assure your grandchild that you are both doing the right thing by praying, and that you must trust God to answer your prayers in his own wise timing.

3. Read 1 John 3:16–18 and James 2:14–18. Consider how giving to meet the needs of others is a testimony of genuine faith in Jesus Christ. Consider possible ways you may be able to help your grandchild's parents—your own child and

their spouse—financially. Seeing your child and their spouse face the challenge of disability can be difficult. But if you support them, you will be helping your grandchild. When your adult child faces a great challenge, ask them to share the details in confidence. At the end of the conversation, ask if you can pray with them about the challenge. While keeping confidence, reassure your offspring that you are praying for them. Writing, emailing, or texting reminders that you are praying will provide parents with encouragement in the face of trials.

4. Read 1 Corinthians 12:12–26. Think about God's design of the church to include those who are "weaker," and how you can engage others in ministering to your grandchild and their parents. It takes a family whose home is connected to a church to raise a child well. You and your grandchild's parents cannot raise your grandchild with a disability alone. What is more, do not rob other people in your family and your church from the blessing of being a part of your grandchild's life. There is enough blessing to go around!

5. Read Philippians 1:1–11. The book of Philippians is a wonderful example of a letter written for the

purpose of encouragement and affirmation. Write your grandchild a special letter. One kind of letter could be for your grandchild to receive after you have departed to heaven. I do not mean for this suggestion to be sad or frightening. I would like you to find great joy by encouraging, comforting, even correcting wayward grandchildren into their future. You can grandparent in powerful ways through your own words written to be read another day. After all, your grandchildren will experience many of the same challenges and frustrations, failures, and heartbreaks as you have in life and from which you have learned. And if your grandchild has a disability, talking about that in sensitive ways may provide strength and courage for a lifetime. You might consider picking one or two issues that you already see your grandchild struggle with and that you are passionate about helping your grandchild get through. Your words will live on in the memory of your grandchild for life. Most importantly, tell your grandchild about your love for Christ and your personal commitment to live an obedient life. Put the letter with other documents that will be read after your passing. If this exercise sounds like it may be too difficult, put it aside to finish for another day. You can do this, and you'll be glad that you did it. Your grandchild will treasure your nurture beyond the grave.

Where Can I Get More Help?

The Legacy Grandparenting Summit, an annual conference for grandparents conducted by Pastor Chuck Swindoll. Visit www.legacycoalition.com/summit.

MacArthur, John, *Safe in the Arms of God: Truth from Heaven about the Death of a Child* (Nashville: Thomas Nelson, 2003). This little book will provide sound biblical comfort and instruction to parents and grandparents who must say goodbye to a child, for a while, due to the child's death.

Mulvihill, Josh, *Biblical Grandparenting: Exploring God's Design for Disciple-Making and Passing Faith to Future Generations* (Grand Rapids: Bethany House, 2016 [revised 2018]). This careful piece of research addresses the topic of biblical grandparenting. Based on the author's doctoral dissertation, the research methodology, documentation, and detailed arguments are not written for the casual reader. The author calls for special grandparenting of a grandchild with a disability.

Towns, Ruth and Elmer, "Grandparents in the Bible: What They Can Teach Us about Influencing Children" (unpublished manuscript, 2003, available at http://docplayer.net/31270766-Grandparents-in-the-bible-what-they-can-teach-us-about-influencing-children.html). This resource was published as Elmer L. and Ruth Towns, *Great Lessons and Grand Blessings: Discover How Grandparents Can Inspire and Transform Their Grandchildren* (Self-published, ChurchGrowth.org, 2015), and has a companion tool, Elmer L. Towns, *Great Lessons and Grand Blessings: Grandparents of the Bible Offer Wisdom for Today; Study Guide* (Shippensburg, PA: Destiny Image Publishers, 2016). It is an encouraging biographical study of select grandparents in the Bible.

Tripp, Tedd, *Shepherding a Child's Heart* (Wapwallopen, PA: Shepherd Press, 2005 [revised and expanded 2009]). This timeless classic, although written primarily for parents, will guide grandparents in the spiritual priorities of nurturing spiritual growth in a child. Also see Tedd Tripp, *Shepherding a Child's Heart: Parent's Handbook* (Wapwallopen, PA: Shepherd Press, 2001), and Tedd and Margy Tripp, *Instructing a Child's Heart* (Wapwallopen, PA: Shepherd Press, 2008).

Endnotes

1 Rick Langer, "Disability, Calling and 'A Kind of Life Imposed on Man,'" in Joni Eareckson Tada and Steve Bundy, Joni and Friends, *Beyond Suffering Study Guide* (Agoura Hills, CA: Christian Institute on Disability, 2011).

2 Os Guinness, *The Call: Finding and Fulfilling the Central Purpose of Your Life* (Nashville: Thomas Nelson, 2003), 235.

3 Cited in H. C. Leopold, *Exposition of the Psalms* (Grand Rapids: Baker, 1959), 895.

4 Josh Mulvihill, *Biblical Grandparenting: Exploring God's Design, Culture's Messages, and Disciple-Making Methods to Pass Faith to Future Generations* (Chaska, MN: At Family, 2016), 119–126.

5 Dave Deuel, "'Devote Yourself to the Reading': 1 Timothy 4:13," *Evangelical Action Annual* (2010): 12–19.

6 Nils Shupak, "Learning Methods in Ancient Israel," *Vetus Testamentum* 53 (2003): 418.

7 Wendy Widder, *"To Teach" in Ancient Israel: A Cognitive Linguistic Study of a Biblical Hebrew Lexical Set*, BZAW 456 (Berlin: de Gruyter, 2014), 194–195.

8 Augustine, *Confessions*, 1.xiv.23 (398 AD).

9 One very helpful children's Bible which accomplishes this is *The Jesus Storybook Bible* by Sally Lloyd-Jones (Grand Rapids: Zondervan, 2007).

10 Z. Ben Barak, "Meribaal and the System of Land Grants in Ancient Israel," *Biblica* 62 (1981): 73–91.

11 Parents and grandparents should read and remain acquainted with Tedd Tripp's book *Shepherding a Child's Heart* (see the Tripp entry under "Where Can I Get More Help?").

It is our great pleasure at Joni & Friends International Disability Center to endorse this mini-book, *Help! My Grandchild has a Disability*, produced by Shepherd Press. We pray this resource will bless you in your journey.

Joni & Friends is answering the call in the Gospel of Luke, chapter 14, "invite the poor, the crippled, the lame, the blind, and you will be blessed.... make them come in so my house will be full." Our mission at Joni & Friends is to communicate the gospel and equip Christ-honoring churches worldwide to evangelize and disciple people affected by disabilities.

We present the gospel of Jesus Christ to all people affected by disability and their families who are served through our programs around the world. We train, disciple, and mentor people affected by disability to exercise their gifts of leadership and service in their churches and communities. Visit us at https://www.joniandfriends.org/ministries/ to learn about all our ministries, such as Wheels for the World, Family Retreats, and radio and television ministries, and to find an area ministry office near you.

Contact Joni & Friends

- Visit our website, www.joniandfriends.org.
- For help and inspiration, visit https://www.joniandfriends.org/help-inspiration/.
- To find out how you can get involved, visit https://www.joniandfriends.org/support-us/.

Books in the Help! series include...

Help! He's Struggling with Pornography
Help! Someone I Love Has Been Abused
Help! My Toddler Rules the House
Help! Someone I Love Has Cancer
Help! I Want to Change
Help! My Spouse Has Been Unfaithful
Help! Someone I Love Has Alzheimer's
Help! I Have Breast Cancer
Help! I'm a Slave to Food
Help! My Teen Struggles With Same-Sex Attractions
Help! She's Struggling With Pornography
Help! I Can't Get Motivated
Help! I'm a Single Mom
Help! I'm Confused About Dating
Help! I'm In a Painful Marriage
Help! Disability Pressures Our Marriage
Help! I'm Drowning in Debt
Help! My Teen is Rebellious
Help! I'm Depressed
Help! I'm Living With Terminal Illness
Help! I Feel Ashamed
Help! I Want to Model Submission in Marriage
Help! I Can't Handle All These Trials
Help! I Can't Forgive
Help! My Anger is Out of Control
Help! My Friend is Suicidal
Help! I'm in a Conflict
Help! I'm Being Deployed
Help! I've Been Traumatized by Combat
Help! I'm So Lonely
Help! My Kids Are Viewing Pornography
Help! I Need a Church
Help! I'm Anxious
Help! My Parents Abused Me When I was a Kid

More titles in preparation

For current listing go to: www.shepherdpress.com/lifeline

About Shepherd Press Publications

- » They are gospel driven.
- » They are heart focused.
- » They are life changing.

Our Invitation to You

We passionately believe that what we are publishing can be of benefit to you, your family, your friends, and your work colleagues. So we are inviting you to join our online mailing list so that we may reach out to you with news about our latest and forthcoming publications, and with special offers.

Visit:

www.shepherdpress.com/newsletter

and provide your name and email address.